KATE MIDDLETON

REAL-LIFE PRINCESS

Peachtree

KATIE LAJINESS

Big Buddy Books

An Imprint of Abdo Publishing
abdopublishing.com

BIG
BUDDY POP BIOGRAPHIES

abdopublishing.com

Published by Abdo Publishing, a division of ABDO, PO Box 398166, Minneapolis, Minnesota 55439.
Copyright © 2016 by Abdo Consulting Group, Inc. International copyrights reserved in all countries.
No part of this book may be reproduced in any form without written permission from the publisher.
Big Buddy Books™ is a trademark and logo of Abdo Publishing.

Printed in the United States of America, North Mankato, Minnesota.
102015
012016

Cover Photo: Samir Hussein/Getty Images.
Interior Photos: ASSOCIATED PRESS (pp. 6, 9, 13, 15, 17, 19, 25, 23, 29); Richard Heathcote/Getty
    Images (p. 11); KGC-178/STAR MAX/Ipx (p. 21); Max Mumby/Indigo/Getty Images (p. 31);
    JONATHAN NACKSTRAND/AFP/Getty Images (p. 9); © NY Post/Splash News/Corbis (p. 17);
    Shutterstock.com (p. 27); © Splash News/Splash News/Corbis (p. 21); © Martio Testino /Art
    Partner/Getty Images (p. 23); WPA Pool/Getty Images (p. 5).

Coordinating Series Editor: Tamara L. Britton
Contributing Editor: Marcia Zappa
Graphic Design: Jenny Christensen

Library of Congress Cataloging-in-Publication Data

Lajiness, Katie, author.
  Kate Middleton / Katie Lajiness.
      pages cm. -- (Big buddy pop biographies)
  Includes index.
  ISBN 978-1-68078-055-0
1. Catherine, Duchess of Cambridge, 1982---Juvenile literature. 2. Princesses--Great Britain--Biog-
raphy--Juvenile literature. I. Title.
  DA591.A45W5557 2016
  941.086'12092--dc23
  [B]
                              2015033045

CONTENTS

REAL ROYALTY

Kate Middleton is part of England's royal family. She is married to Prince William, Duke of Cambridge. He is second in line to be king of England.

Many people think of Kate as a princess. But, her main title is the Duchess of Cambridge. As a duchess, she attends important events and does **charity** work.

SNAPSHOT

NAME:
Catherine Elizabeth
"Kate" Middleton

BIRTHDAY:
January 9, 1982

BIRTHPLACE:
Reading, England

OFFICIAL TITLES:
Duchess of Cambridge,
Countess of Strathearn,
Baroness Carrickfergus

FAMILY TIES

Catherine Elizabeth "Kate" Middleton was born in Reading, England, on January 9, 1982. Kate's parents are Michael and Carole Middleton. Her younger sister is Philippa, or Pippa. Her younger brother is James.

Kate's parents met while working for an airline.

WHERE IN THE WORLD?

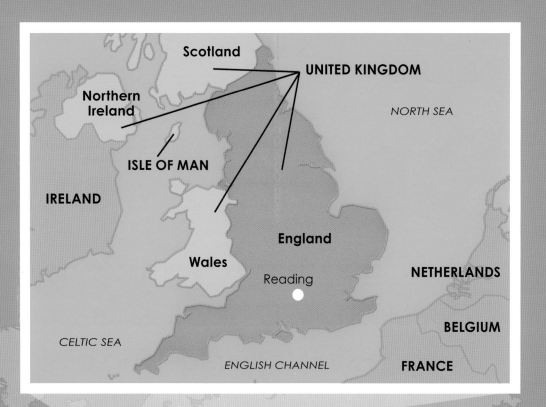

Scotland

UNITED KINGDOM

Northern Ireland

NORTH SEA

ISLE OF MAN

IRELAND

England

Reading

Wales

NETHERLANDS

BELGIUM

CELTIC SEA

ENGLISH CHANNEL

FRANCE

GROWING UP

Kate grew up in an ordinary family. They lived in Bucklebury, England. Kate's parents owned a successful party-planning business.

Growing up, Kate attended boarding schools in the English countryside. These are schools where students can live during the school term. Kate was a good student. She was also a talented field hockey and tennis player.

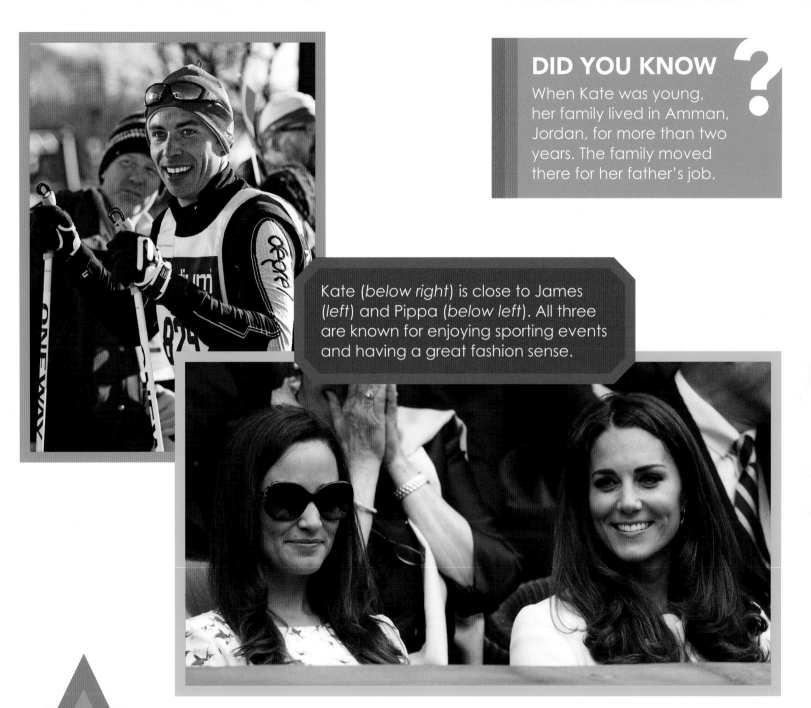

DID YOU KNOW ?

When Kate was young, her family lived in Amman, Jordan, for more than two years. The family moved there for her father's job.

Kate (*below right*) is close to James (*left*) and Pippa (*below left*). All three are known for enjoying sporting events and having a great fashion sense.

MEETING A PRINCE

In 2001, Kate began studying art history at the University of Saint Andrews in Scotland. There, she met Prince William. They soon became close friends.

After **graduating** in 2005, Kate worked as a buyer at a clothing company. She also helped out with her parents' business. During this time, Kate and William remained close.

Kate and William enjoy similar hobbies such as traveling and sports. They spend time skiing and watching tennis, rugby, and polo.

A ROYAL WEDDING

In 2010, William asked Kate to marry him. The couple's royal wedding took place in London, England, on April 29, 2011. They were married at Westminster Abbey.

DID YOU KNOW?
William asked Kate to marry him while they were on vacation in Africa!

After their wedding, the queen gave William and Kate the titles of Duke and Duchess of Cambridge. This was a special honor.

Kate and William's wedding drew much attention. About 1 million people lined the streets to watch. Around the world, an estimated 2 billion people watched the wedding on television and the Internet.

DID YOU KNOW?
On July 29, 1981, more than 750 million people around the world watched Prince William's parents get married.

After their wedding, Kate and William rode through London in a carriage. William's parents rode in the same carriage on their wedding day!

A NEW LIFE

After the wedding, Kate's life became even busier! She started attending royal events including garden parties. She also started **representing** the royal family at **charity** activities and national sporting events.

As part of the royal family, Kate lives a **privileged** life. She carries out royal duties in England and overseas. People bow or **curtsy** when they meet her.

DID YOU KNOW
The royal family has a team of guards to keep them safe.

Kate often attends garden parties at Buckingham Palace. A garden party is a fancy gathering outdoors.

In 2014, Kate and William met Jay-Z (*left*) and Beyoncé (*second from left*) at a basketball game in New York City, New York.

CHARITIES

Part of Kate's royal duties includes working with **charities**. She has worked with UNICEF to help children all over the world. This group provides health care, education, and food.

Kate also helped establish the Royal Foundation. This group helps many different causes. One of these supports outdoor trips for children. These help kids learn new skills and believe in themselves.

In 2015, Kate decorated a mug as part of a project to raise money for East Anglia's Children's Hospices. This charity helps children with serious illnesses.

FASHION FORWARD

Kate is known as a fashion icon. So, reporters often take pictures of what she wears. Her style is seen in magazines and on **websites**.

Kate's style changes depending on the occasion. Sometimes, she wears dresses made just for her. Other times, she wears simple pieces such as jeans and T-shirts.

Kate's outfits are often remarkable. At a 2015 Wimbledon tennis match, fans and reporters noticed Kate's red dress.

In England, people commonly wear fancy hats for special events. So, Kate is often seen in one.

PRINCE GEORGE

Prince George Alexander Louis was born on July 22, 2013, in London. He is third in line for the **throne** after his grandfather and father.

George was **baptized** on October 23, 2013. William has called his son "a little monkey" because George is always running and climbing on things!

George (*above*) looks much like his father did at his age (*right*).

PRINCESS CHARLOTTE

Princess Charlotte Elizabeth Diana was born on May 2, 2015, in London. She is fourth in line for the **throne**.

Charlotte was **baptized** on July 5, 2015. She has five **godparents** to guide her throughout her life. Her godparents are close friends of William and Kate.

In July 2015, the royal family gathered to celebrate Charlotte's baptism. The event was held at the Saint Mary Magdalene Church.

FAMILY LIFE

Kate and her family enjoy spending time at the royal family's homes. Their main residence is Anmer Hall, their country home. Still, they often visit London to attend events.

When Kate and William have time to themselves, they like to vacation in Africa and the Caribbean. They also travel the world for official visits. The family has a **nanny** for the children while Kate and William are busy.

Kate and William also have an apartment in Kensington Palace in London. The palace dates back to 1605. Parts of it are open for public tours.

DID YOU KNOW ?

Kate loves sailing. In summer 2015, she attended America's Cup. But, the event was cancelled for bad weather.

BUZZ

As the mother of two young children, Kate balances family life with her royal duties. She continues to **represent** the royal family with exceptional grace. Everyone is excited to see what's next for Kate and her royal family.

In 2015, Kate and William attended the Wimbledon tennis matches.

GLOSSARY

baptize to dip in water or sprinkle water on as a part of the ceremony of receiving into the Christian church.

charity a group or a fund that helps people in need.

curtsy a formal way a woman greets an important person by placing one foot slightly behind the other and bending her knees.

godparent a person selected by a child's parents to provide spiritual guidance.

graduate (GRA-juh-wayt) to complete a level of schooling.

nanny a person who is paid to care for a young child usually in the child's home.

privileged having more things and a better chance in life than most people.

represent to act for or in place of.

throne the position of a king or queen.

website a group of World Wide Web pages usually containing links to each other and made available online by an individual, company, or organization.

WEBSITES

To learn more about Pop Biographies, visit **booklinks.abdopublishing.com**.
These links are routinely monitored and updated to provide
the most current information available.

INDEX